Gerbils

Based on
material supplied by
D. G. Robinson, Jr.

This book originally appeared as *Know Your Gerbils*. It has been updated and enhanced with beautiful full-color photographs for this new TFH edition.

Distributed in the UNITED STATES by T.F.H. Publications, Inc., 211 West Sylvania Avenue, Neptune City, NJ 07753; in CANADA by H & L Pet Supplies Inc., 27 Kingston Crescent, Kitchener, Ontario N2B 2T6; Rolf C. Hagen Ltd., 3225 Sartelon Street, Montreal 382 Quebec; in ENGLAND by T.F.H. Publications Limited, 4 Kier Park, Ascot, Berkshire SL5 7DS; in AUSTRALIA AND THE SOUTH PACIFIC by T.F.H. (Australia) Pty. Ltd., Box 149, Brookvale 2100 N.S.W., Australia; in NEW ZEALAND by Ross Haines & Son, Ltd., 18 Monmouth Street, Grey Lynn, Auckland 2 New Zealand; in SINGAPORE AND MALAYSIA by MPH Distributors (S) Pte., Ltd., 601 Sims Drive, # 03/07/21, Singapore 1438; in the PHILIPPINES by Bio-Research, 5 Lippay Street, San Lorenzo Village, Makati Rizal; in SOUTH AFRICA by Multipet Pty. Ltd., 30 Turners Avenue, Durban 4001. Published by T.F.H. Publications Inc., Ltd. the British Crown Colony of Hong Kong.

Contents

Introduction, 5

What Is a Gerbil?, 6
The Mongolian Gerbil, 7; Skimming, 8;
Gerbils in the Wild, 8

Choosing Your Gerbil, 11
How Many Gerbils?, 11; Sexing, 11;
Age, 11; Health, 12; On the Road, 12

Housing, 13
Steel Cages, 13; Plastic Cages, 13; An
Aquarium, 15; Hamster Cage, 15;
Wood, 16; Other Possibilities, 16; Lots
of Elbow Room, 25; Bedding, 25;
Water, 26; Exercise, 28; Nest Box, 28;
Toys, 28; Lost Gerbils, 28

Environment, 32
Indoors or Out?, 32; Keep It Cool—But
Not Too Cool!, 32; Humidity, 33;
Light or Darkness?, 33; Noise, 33;
Generally Speaking, 34

You Are What You Eat, 35
Basic Diet, 37; Those Little Extras, 37

Handling and Training, 40
Biting, 41; Children, 41; Eating from
Your Hand, 41; Playtime, 42; The
Basis of Training, 42; Escapees, 43

And Baby Makes Three, 45
Arranged Marriage, 45; Pair Them
Young, 46; The Blessed Event, 46;
Delivery Signs, 47; Littering, 47; Post-
partum Heat, 48; Cannibalism, 48

Growth and Development, 49
Mama's Duties, 49; Papa's Duties, 49;
The Neglected Litter, 49; As They
Grow, 50; Weaning, 51; Separate the
Sexes, 51

Keep Him Healthy, 52
Delivery Problems, 52; Tyzzer's Disease,
53; Vitamin Deficiency, 53; Seizures, 55;
Ulcerations, 55; Hair Loss, 56; External
Parasites, 65; Miscellaneous, 66; Keep
Him Clean, 66

A Friend to Science, 67
The Unique Gerbil, 67; Cholesterol and
Heart Disease, 67; Hormone Studies,
68; Neurology, 68; Dentistry, 68;
Tissue Transplants, 68; Psychological
Studies, 69; And That's Not All, 69

Gerbils in the Classroom, 70
Public Housing, 70; The Scientific
Approach, 71; Plan Ahead, 72;
Experiments with Food, 72; Bodily
Functions, 73; Activity, 74; Be
Observant, 74; The Maze, 75

Here's to the Gerbil, 76

Suggested Reading, 77

Index,

Introduction

A little animal that was virtually unknown except to scientists before the 1960's is rapidly overtaking the hamster, guinea pig, and mouse in popularity as a children's pet. The gerbil is a lively little creature, clean and easy to care for—it's no wonder that he has become a favorite in homes and classrooms around the world. His climb to popularity wherever he has been introduced is little less than phenomenal.

With the wealth of material written about gerbils in the last few years, it might seem there would be very little new to say. Before starting this book, however, I did a little checking with pet experts.

Much to my surprise, I found that a great deal of new information had surfaced recently—information I am delighted to make available here.

With all that we've learned, there's still a great deal left to discover, but the information here, you may be sure, is reliable. With this as a guide you can be certain that your pets will receive the attention they deserve, and you will enjoy them all the more, secure in the knowledge that you are doing the right thing.

*Facing page: The original habitat of our common pet gerbil is Mongolia—one of the driest places in the world. **Below:** Gerbils accept sunflower seeds anytime; they are a real treat for them.*

What Is a Gerbil?

Travelers across the arid plains of Asia, Africa, and eastern Europe, if they are sharp of eye, might spot some of the little rodents common to these areas. When the animals emerge from their burrows, where they protect themselves from the heat of the day and the chill of the night, they scurry about, feeding on roots and plants. With water scarce in these regions, the animals have developed special body mechanisms that not only help conserve the water in their bodies but also extract moisture from their food. Zoologists have divided these rodents into various groups such as gerbils, jirds, sand rats, antelope rats, and desert rats. Until fairly recently they received very little world attention, although scientists have known them for many years.

The different species of gerbils are of various sizes, with the largest about the size of a house rat. Their fur is often brownish on top with a lighter-colored underside. They are distinguishable as rodents by their narrow front teeth (incisors).

A gerbil drinks very little water. Get the smallest gravity-feed bottle available.

What Is a Gerbil?

Enlarged eardrum sacs in the skull provide them with excellent hearing, and their elongated hindlegs make them agile jumpers.

The Mongolian Gerbil

In 1935 a research institute in Tokyo received a shipment of 20 pairs of a species of rodent from eastern Mongolia. These were our own little gerbils, *Meriones unguiculatus,* which seemed to offer considerable promise for medical research. It took a number of years to work up a breeding stock, but by 1949 a colony was established in an experimental laboratory in Japan for further testing. In 1954, 11 pairs of gerbils, descendants of the original 20 pairs, were sent to Dr. Victor Schwentker, a well-known geneticist at the West Foundation in Brant Lake, New York. Of the 11 pairs he received, he successfully induced five females and four males to breed. These were the basis for a consistently reproducing colony from which, within a decade, thousands of gerbils were bred. Soon, the gerbil became the fastest-growing small pet in popularity in the country.

Those who worked with gerbils in laboratories quickly discovered that they are easy to handle; are active during the day; seldom bite; have no special food or housing demands; drink very little water; and are virtually odorless. Because of their amiable disposition, they came to be called "gentle gerbils," and these virtues were publicized not only through the press and television but also via the fastest medium of them all, the children's grapevine. Gerbils became a familiar sight in elementary classrooms, and by 1965 gerbils were challenging hamsters as a favorite pet among children in the six- to ten-year age group. Their popularity has remained consistently high since then.

Although so many people have kept them and so much has been written about them, there are still many misconceptions to be cleared up. First of all, the correct name is not just "gerbil"; the little fellow we're interested in is the *Mongolian gerbil.* However, because it's the only gerbil well-known in the United States, we can get away with calling him simply "gerbil." The word means "jerboa-like"—the jerboa is a similar but larger rodent native to the Middle East and parts of North Africa. Besides being larger, the jerboa has considerably longer hindlegs and leaps like a

What Is a Gerbil?

miniature kangaroo. The Arabic term for jerboa is *yarbu;* from this came the Latin *gerbo.* Because of their physical resemblance to jerboas, when gerbils were first classified scientifically they were called *gerbillus,* which means "little jerboa" or "jerboa-like." In French this word became *gerbille,* which led to the English "gerbil." So, the "g" in "gerbil" should be pronounced softly (as in the word germ), since it is a soft "g" in the French.

In spite of their close resemblance to the jerboa, the gerbil's closest relatives are actually hamsters and voles such as the meadow mouse and deer mouse.

Your gerbil will grow to a length of about 4 inches, with his tail almost as long again. He will weigh 3 to 4 ounces. At first glance a gerbil appears to be darker on the back and lighter on the sides, but this is an optical illusion. Actually, each hair of the coat has a white or gray base, centerband of yellow or brown, and a black tip. Unlike rats and mice, which have hairless tails, and hamsters, which have hardly any tails, the gerbil has a long furred tail with a dark tuft at the end. His hindlegs are long and strong, his feet are furry, and there are five dark claws on each foot. The skull is rather broad. One of

his outstanding features is his eyes. They protrude slightly and are large, dark, sparkling, and alert.

Skimming

There is a narrow, flat sebaceous (oil-secreting) gland pad on the midline of the abdomen. The gland remains small in the female but in the male enlarges at puberty and turns orange. The male "skims" or marks his territory with the secretion from this gland by rubbing his abdomen over the area to be marked.

Gerbils in the Wild

In their natural habitat, gerbils live in groups or colonies. A typical burrow complex may cover a surface area of about 10 by 14 feet, with six or seven 2-inch diameter entrances to a main tunnel, which can be 10 to 12 feet long and slope downward as far as 2 feet. The main tunnel has several branches and may be arranged in levels.

At about the midpoint of the tunnel, the gerbil hollows out a nesting room, lines it with chewed blades of grass or grain, and then encircles it with whole leaves. In

What Is a Gerbil?

their nests, gerbils may produce as many as four litters a year with four to six young in each. (There is no particular breeding season.) The providential gerbil also hollows out one or two food storage rooms near the nest. All spring and summer he is busy not only digging and repairing his nest and rearing his young, but also filling his granaries with seeds and grain. By the time cold weather comes he will have stored away enough food to last until the next growing season.

As protection against predators, gerbils in the wild build extensive burrows with small and inconspicuous openings.

Choosing Your Gerbil

Although many burrowing animals excavate a little toilet, gerbils do not have a fixed spot for their droppings. This is probably due to their water-conserving ways—their droppings are very dry, and there is very little urine.

How long do gerbils live in the wild? We don't really know; the best estimate is about two years.

It is really something to see a gerbil dig! Those sharp-clawed forefeet flash rapidly as he excavates, while the powerful hindlegs kick loose soil to the rear. The fur pads on his feet act like snowshoes to keep him from sinking into the soft sand. The head operates like a bulldozer. Once the nest is excavated, the bedding material is carried in by mouth.

When choosing your new pet, you'll find color selection your main problem—friend gerbil now comes in several colors. Other than this, there is altogether very little difference in the general physical characteristics of gerbils. Normally males are larger than females of the same age. Differences in size and weight can be quite marked in the wild even among gerbils of the same age and sex, but through selective breeding in the gerbilry and laboratory, they are being greatly reduced. Things you need to consider when setting out to make your purchase are how many gerbils to buy and their state of health.

A well constructed and safe exercise wheel. Not all exercise wheels are safe for gerbils.

Choosing Your Gerbil

How Many Gerbils?

Ask the man who owns one, and he'll tell you that these sociable little fellows seem lonely when kept by themselves. Of course, if you get opposite sexes, be prepared to care for, rear, and eventually give nature's blessings away to responsible pet lovers.

If you'd rather your pets didn't breed, then your best bet is two females—they'll get along better than two males. (Sometimes when females are kept together one or both may experience a pseudo- or false pregnancy. There is nothing you can do except to leave them alone and they'll recover.) To make sure they get along well, try to obtain them from a group that has been living together—even better, from the same litter. If you are going to put two strange gerbils together, try to do so before they are ten weeks of age.

If you still feel, however, that just one is best for you, you can take your pick of either sex. Just be sure to give your new friend plenty of attention, a variety of foods, and a selection of toys to indulge his insatiable curiosity. A lone gerbil with nothing to occupy his mind may very well become irritable.

Sexing

Most young animals tend to resemble the female of the species, and this is also true of gerbils. In mature animals, the distance from the anus to the external genital organs is about half an inch for the male and a quarter of an inch for the female. This extreme difference in adults makes it easy to sex one by itself, but when selecting a pair of youg gerbils, it is best to examine several of them. Then, by picking the one with the greatest and the one with the least distance between the two openings, you can be reasonably certain you'll have a pair.

Another way to sex adults is by looking at them from above or from one side. You'll see that the male's rump is more tapered and tufted than the female's, and if you turn them over you'll find a distinctly dark patch around the males scrotal area.

Age

The age of your new pet is not really too important. Problems may arise, though, when older strangers are put together. This is almost certain to result in bickering or even

Choosing Your Gerbil

serious injury to one or both. Better opt for young gerbils, somewhere between four and nine weeks of age. It's lots of fun to see them grow and to watch their antics—they're as active and playful as kittens.

Health

Gerbils are so healthy that most or all of those you wean will live to the ripe old age of about three years with even reasonable care. Of course, there are a few obvious indications of injuries or illness, but these are rare. Look out for partially closed eyes, a stubby tail or one with a kink or knot in it, or sores near the rump or the head.

As a rule, if the animal has a well-filled-out body, glossy coat, bright eyes, dry nose, and is active and alert, you can be fairly sure that he is in good health. Just remember that a gerbil is not *always* active—he sometimes likes to rest. Also, his coat could be ruffled from sleeping or from the high humidity found in most petshops.

On the Road

Gerbils are great travelers, whether they're going cross-country

Junior will certainly appreciate the help and advice of Mom and Dad for setting up the housing kit just purchased.

by train or just being brought home from the petshop by car. Just make certain that the container in which they travel is ventilated and escape-proof. No car owner appreciates a gerbil's crawling up into a seat and chewing away at the upholstery!

Once you've gotten your gerbil home, make sure that he has adequate food, water, and bedding; then just leave him alone for a day—he'll be tired out from so much excitement.

Housing

I If you want your gerbils to be happy, you must provide a home that allows enough room for a pair of lively adults plus offspring. It must be escape-proof and be without projections or cracks to injure the animals. They should be able to look out, but at the same time they must have some shelter to give them privacy.

The enclosure should provide ventilation without drafts, be smooth and moisture-resistant so it can be cleaned easily, and be lightweight but not fragile. Of course it should also be inexpensive. A tall order? Not really, if you combine wood, metal, glass, and plastic for your pets' new dwelling.

A plastic cage especially designed for housing small mammals.

Steel Cages

Most laboratories keep gerbils in rectangular cages of either stainless steel or plastic. The lids provide ventilation through perforations in the stainless steel sheet or by a wire mesh or grid. Often there is a trough built into the lid that doubles as a food hopper and water bottle holder. Stainless steel cages are sturdy and easy to clean, but they are also expensive and provide little visibility for the pet owner. Tin or galvanized steel costs less but will eventually rust, and the rusted areas are difficult to keep clean.

Plastic Cages

Transparent plastic cages are a little better, not only because they are see-through but also because they provide insulation against drafts. In time, though, the plastic may be marred by burrowing, and a hard plastic may crack if dropped. Still, a good-sized plastic sweater storage box can serve as a cage if nothing else is available. It may be used as is just by adding a wire mesh cover with a hole drilled or

Aquariums and terrariums make excellent gerbil cages.

A normal cage can be used for breeding gerbils. It helps, however, to cover three sides of the cage with cardboard to keep down the light and shield the breeders from noise and strange movements.

An all-glass aquarium is probably the best gerbil set-up for commercial breeders, since most petshops sell "leakers" very inexpensively, and the gerbil doesn't care whether the tank leaks or not . . . and neither should you. Be sure to get a top for the aquarium!

Housing

melted through one end for the water bottle tube. Or just prop the bottle up on the lid so that the drinking tube projects into the cage far enough for the animals to reach it.

An Aquarium

Instead of a metal or plastic box, you might substitute an old aquarium; a 10-gallon tank 12 inches high with floor space 20 by 10 inches is fine. You can buy or make a wire mesh top, and you can fashion a piece of wire (an old coat hanger, for instance) into a holder for the water bottle. Your local petshop will provide lights, stands, and other accessories, if necessary.

A variety of housing setups for gerbils is available in your local pet store.

The setup completed and the gerbil installed, it is now time to observe our "guest."

Hamster Cage

Probably the most satisfactory housing you can provide is the metal cage so widely used for hamsters. This is solid sheet metal except for the front, which is a grid of wires or a sheet of glass. If the front is glass, the metal sides must be perforated for ventilation and the glass washed regularly. If you get the wire-front type, it is best to catch anything that may be kicked out. The cage should have an exercise wheel, a clip for attaching a water bottle, a shelf for climbing or shelter, and a removable pan for droppings.

15

Housing

Be sure to cover your cage—unless you enjoy hunting gerbils through the whole house.

to minimize the scattering of bedding. One side or the top should be made of wire mesh for visibility and ventilation. If you put a piece of metal, plastic, or some other hard-surfaced material on the floor, it will be easier to clean. Look out for loose nails or wire ends that can scratch.

Other Possibilities

Gerbil owners have utilized metal tubs, glass fishbowls, and bird cages to house their pets. If you choose one of these, be sure that all openings are securely covered with wire mesh or bars small enough to

Wood

Many people use wood—it's cheap and easy to work with. But it's really not too durable, and of course it's hard to clean. If you must use wood, stick to exterior-grade plywood or tempered hardboard and protect the interior corners against gnawing with wire mesh or sheet metal. Make the sides high enough

Captions for color pages 17-24:

Page 17: Dove-colored female and agouti Canadian white spot male in pre-mating pose. Page 18: Dove female gerbil with her litter. Page 19: Agouti Canadian white spot gerbil with scent gland visible just below front paws. Page 20: A young black gerbil looks expectantly to his owner. Page 21: The white gerbil is a male; the black gerbil is a female. Page 22: Female black gerbil. Page 23: Cinnamon gerbil in typical curious gerbil pose. Page 24: Gerbils mating.

Housing

Looking over some fancy types of gerbil housing in the local petshop.

prevent your pet's sticking his head through.

Whatever your final choice, be sure the floor is solid so that the animals can burrow into the bedding.

Lots of Elbow Room

Don't squeeze your gerbils into a minimal amount of space. Figure about 180 square inches of usable floor space for a pair and their young. A 13- or 14-inch square, for example, or a 10- by 18-inch rectangle, would suffice. The cage should be at least 6 inches high—2 inches for bedding and 4 inches to allow the gerbil to sit up without bumping his head.

Bedding

Gerbils excrete only a few drops of urine daily, and the feces are nearly dry and odorless, so almost any type of bedding material may be used. Just make certain that it is suitable for burrowing and nesting and will not harm the gerbil if he should chew it.

This one is simple, but it's adequate for a single pet gerbil.

Housing

Gerbils are not fussy as to their bedding.

often—every two or three weeks will do. One way of postponing the major cleanup is to occasionally scoop out the most soiled areas and replace them with fresh bedding. Remember that this doesn't preclude the necessity for eventually cleaning all of it out; it merely postpones the chore.

Change the water regularly. Harmful bacteria may be present in stale water.

Wood shavings, wood chips, sawdust, excelsior, sand and soil, ground corn cobs, cardboard, cloth, processed alfalfa, granular cellulose, hay, peanut hulls—any of these or a mixture of several of them will provide satisfactory bedding.

Gerbils love to work over their nesting material, shredding it and carrying around mouthfuls of it as they rearrange their nests, so choose bedding of a size and texture that permits them to carry on this work conveniently. Newspaper is great except for one thing: the ink comes off and stains the animals.

Less enthusiastic house-keepers—like us humans—will welcome the news that it's not necessary to change the bedding too

Housing

Pine wood shavings are inexpensive and easy to replace when soiled.

Water

Many gerbil owners don't give their pets any water at all; they just drop in a piece of carrot or apple or some other moisture-filled fruit or vegetable daily. However, I prefer to let the gerbil make his own choice as to whether or not to drink.

Water is best provided by means of a gravity feed or suck bottle: this is a bottle with a single-hole screw cap rubber stopper fitted in the mouth and a piece of tubing (glass, aluminum, steel, or plastic) about ¼ inch in diameter stuck into the cap so that about 1½ inches protrude. This is filled with water, the top fitted tightly into place, and then hung upside down in the cage or set on the cage with the open end of the tube projecting inside. Air pressure keeps the water at the tip of the nozzle. Don't worry about how the gerbil will learn to use the bottle—he'll soon figure that out for himself.

An adult gerbil will consume only about a thimbleful of water a day, and an 8-ounce bottle will normally last a pair and their young for a week. You'll find yourself refilling the bottle more often just to be sure the water is fresh. If the bottle has to be refilled *too* often, you had better look into the cause—possibly there's a leak in the cap or tube. Also, if the tip of the tube is touching any absorbent material, this will act as a wick and soak up the water.

Housing

Exercise

Gerbils are so active and restless that they get lots of exercise without any special equipment—but they will enjoy an exercise wheel if one is available. (Some keepers feel that the gerbil's long tail may be damaged by a wheel, an opinion to keep in mind if you use a wheel.) You might want to make an inclined disc, which allows the gerbil to run in a more normal posture. To do this, make a wooden disc about 5 inches in diameter and fix a stout bolt or machine screw through the center to serve as an axle. Now mount a piece of copper tubing at an angle on a board platform and stick the protruding end of the screw into the open end of the tubing so that the disc can revolve freely.

Watching a gerbil exercise can be fascinating.

Nest Box

A small metal or wooden box with a 2-inch entrance will do fine as a nest box. Gerbils don't really need them, but they do enjoy them. You can instead provide a small flowerpot or a tin can on its side in which your little chum will curl up and take a nap.

Toys

To keep those teeth busy, give him a piece of wood, a twig, or a clean bone from time to time. Little toys, such as those made for parakeets, will provide him with an endless source of amusement.

Lost Gerbils

Don't let your gerbils run around loose while you're cleaning the

Housing

A gerbil cage with a drawer-type bottom.

The top of this cage can be raised as a unit for cleaning the bottom tray.

Housing

Housing

cage—it's amazing how fast they can vanish into the most unlikely places. Press a bucket or a box into duty, making sure that the animals can't crawl or gnaw their way through. Remember that your gerbil may be tame enough so that he really doesn't want to run away but that hole in the wall or crack under the bed may look awfully inviting to him, and he may have difficulty finding his way back.

Facing page:

A piece of loosely woven fabric is a good source of nesting material.

Right:

Gnawing is a normal activity of a rodent, which is one reason for not using a cage entirely made of wood.

Environment

Once you've decided on a cage for the little fellow, the next consideration is his environment. We keep stessing that gerbils are adaptable, but like all other living creatures, they do like to be comfortable.

An accessory cage and several tubes create a burrow-like environment.

Indoors or Out?

If you live in an area with a mild climate the year around, you might want to keep your gerbil outdoors. However, there are several drawbacks here. Unless you provide some sort of shelter, it's very difficult to protect him from extremes of weather. Wandering cats or dogs will try to get into the cage and, even if they can't make it through the bars, they are liable to make a nervous wreck of your pet. Wild rodents might transfer one of the diseases that are often endemic to them to your own pet. Insects can also present a health problem. And, of course, should your gerbil escape, it would be so much harder to find him again outdoors.

Keep it Cool—But Not Too Cool!

Give your gerbil a lot of bedding and he can tolerate a temperature down to freezing if necessary, although I am sure he would not be too happy. Of course, should the temperature drop too low for too long, reproduction will slow down or even stop; in fact, so might the gerbil—permanently. On the other hand, wide daily variations from about 60°F to about 85°F seem to have no adverse effect. Not that such wide variations are recommended—they are merely mentioned to illustrate the gerbil's adaptability: 70°F to 75°F is probably the best temperature range, one at which the gerbil is comfortable and active.

Look out for direct sunlight through a glass or plastic enslosure or even confinement in direct sunlight. During the summertime

Environment

Spend some time observing gerbils in the dealer's shop before making a purchase.

the heat buildup under those conditions could be enough to injure or even kill our little friend. Remember that when it gets too hot in their natural habitat gerbils go underground into a cool burrow, so always provide shade to which he can retreat, as well as adequate ventilation. (But look out for drafts.)

In the same connection, be careful of radiators; placing a gerbil near a radiator during warm weather when the heat is turned off can result in a cooked gerbil when the steam comes up.

Humidity

Gerbils prefer a dry atmosphere. In fact, their fur will appear matted if there is too much dampness. But don't be alarmed if this should happen after they have piled together for a snooze—this is perfectly normal, and if the situation is rectified, there should be no ill effects. Just give them clean, dry bedding to absorb the excess moisture.

Light or Darkness?

Light or the lack of it does not seem to make much difference to the gerbil. One scientist tested this by keeping two colonies under different light conditions. One was kept artificially on a constant 13-hour day, and the other was exposed to the normal fluctuations of daylight. The difference in the lighting did not seem to affect their breeding cycle at all. It is probable, however, that they would prefer not to be directly exposed to too strong a light for too long a period of time.

Noise

In the remote desert areas gerbils inhabitat, there is really very little

There are no air circulation problems in this type of cage. However, be sure to set the cage in a place without drafts.

medicines, gas stoves, and so on. If you install an electric light in the cage, don't place the electric cord where the gerbils might gnaw it. If the exercise wheel squeaks, use vegetable oil to oil it, not petroleum, which could give your pet a stomachache if he should lick it.

Animals have a built-in mechanism called circadian rhythm that allows them to judge the passage of time quite accurately. If you set certain times for feeding, cleaning, and handling and stick to the schedule whenever possible, they will soon anticipate these activities and fare better.

noise. Possibly an occasional thunderstorm or a passing jet is all that ever disturbs their peace. A gerbil's hearing is very keen, yet in spite of this, they do not seem to be bothered much by noise in captivity. So don't be overly concerned about normal household noises such as appliances, tools, or music—these are all tolerated.

Generally Speaking

You should be aware of the dangers of paints, dyes, petroleum products, insect sprays, fumes,

Set the cage in a safe place, out of reach from cats or dogs that you may have.

You Are What You Eat

Because hamsters have been known so much longer than gerbils, thousands of papers have been published on the results of experiments with hamsters in the past 35 years, yet less than 3% deal with nutrition. For gerbils even less data is available. Papers reporting studies of their nutrition are few and far between.

The usual method for testing the nutritional requirements of animals is to set up various groups and feed each group a diet lacking in one

For variety, give tidbits of fresh vegetables or fruit from your own kitchen.

The food requirements of gerbils are not too different from those of other small mammals.

specific nutritional component (a certain vitamin or mineral, for example). If the animal survives this diet without any apparent ill effects, it is then bred and the young are raised on the same diet. Only after several generations is it reasonable to conclude that the component is not required in the diet. As you can see, this can take quite a long time, and as gerbils have been popular for only a relatively short time, this work has yet to be completed.

On the basis of studies made so far, it would seem that gerbils will thrive as well on food put out for hamsters, mice, and rats as they will on food specifically prepared for gerbils. Fortunately, gerbils have very catholic tastes—they'll try almost anything.

You Are What You Eat

The strong maternal instinct of a new mother is very evident here. If molested, this female gerbil will not hesitate to bite the intruder.

You Are What You Eat

Basic Diet

If you want to do it the easy way, stick to the commercial pelleted feeds made for mice, rats, and hamsters. These pellets are a convenient size, eliminate a lot of waste, and are acceptable to both adults and their young. Don't buy too much at once, and keep it in a cool, dry place to avoid deterioration. A pair of gerbils will eat only a few ounces a week.

The U.S. Department of Agriculture requires a statement on the labels of animal feeds showing, among other things, the fat and protein content of the food. Most rodent pellets contain about 4 to 8% fat and 18 to 24% protein. Gerbil breeders tend to believe that low-fat, high-protein feeds give the best breeding results. So before you feed any pellets, check the fat content on the label and select one of the lower fat-content brands—particularly if it is to be fed over a long period of time.

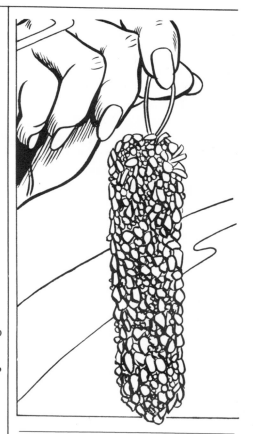

Your gerbil can also survive on a diet of mixed bird seeds.

Those Little Extras

There are lots of dry foods that can be given as supplements or treats. Seeds (such as sunflower, pumpkin, squash, or the mixture of seeds prepared for wild birds), corn, oats, barley, oatmeal, cornflakes, bread, popcorn, potato chips, crackers, dog biscuits, and peanuts are just a few possibilities. Don't overdo the sunflower seeds—they're about 20% fat and only about 10% protein.

You Are What You Eat

Wild gerbils eat fruits, vegetables, and greens, so you can supplement the diet with bits of lettuce, carrots, apple, cabbage, kale, alfalfa, grass, pear, melon, dandelion, clover, cucumber, celery, asparagus, parsley, escarole, potato, tomato, peas, blueberries, or grapes. But be careful: all greens, fruits, and vegetables should be washed well to remove any sprays or insecticides.

You will know whether your gerbil is doing well with the food you give. Improper food will remain uneaten, and spoiled food will make it sick.

Pelleted food is clean, convenient, and nutritious.

Offer greens in moderation a few times a week, and get rid of leftovers before they go bad.

If introducing new foods results in diarrhea, discontinue them for awhile and feed only the dry diet. You can try again later on by introducing very small amounts very gradually until the gerbil has adjusted to the change.

One veterinarian claims excellent breeding results by keeping a mixture of hamster and guinea pig pellets available at all times and supplementing these with bits of

You Are What You Eat

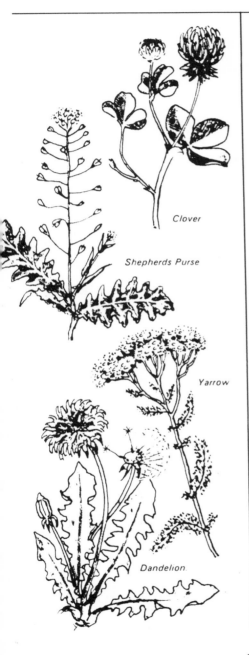

Clover

Shepherds Purse

Yarrow

Dandelion

carrot, lettuce, cabbage, or apple three times a week, plus three mealworms per animal once a week. Gerbils will eat other insects as well, but authorities do not recommend feeding meat regularly, as gerbils are basically vegetarians.

Whatever supplements you give your pets, always keep some pellets available for them to nibble. Put them into a dish, where they'll stay clean and you can easily see when the supply is running low. Or make a little hopper out of ½-inch wire mesh or wire grids about 7/16 inch apart. This can be set into the cover with the top open for easy refilling. Just be sure that it's low enough so that the gerbils, especially the young ones, can reach it. They'll chew the pellets right through the wire mesh.

Gerbils will eat some edible plants found in the wild. These foods, however, should be free of organic and inorganic pollution.

Handling and Training

You don't need a great deal of skill and experience to tame a gerbil. Be gentle, don't move suddenly, add a dash of patience, and you'll have no trouble. Most animals to whom you are a stranger will retreat to the back of the cage when you open the door. Not the gerbil—he's too curious about what is going on. More likely than not, he'll climb right up onto your hand and set about exploring it.

Until you are accustomed to handling your gerbils, the easiest way to pick them up is to use the handle provided by nature: grasp the tail near the base with your thumb and forefinger and lift. It won't take long for your pet to become used to your hand. Don't just reach out and grab him—let him see your hand first. Gain his confidence by using calm and deliberate movements. Stroke the top of his head with your forefinger, and if he runs away don't chase him. Wait for him to quiet down, and then gently approach him again.

When you have gained more confidence, you can either scoop your gerbil up in the palm of your hand or you can lift him by curling your hand loosely around his back with your thumb and forefinger around his neck. Be gentle. Don't squeeze, or he'll struggle to escape.

And never, never try to lift a gerbil by the tip of his tail. The skin there is very thin and slippery, and you don't want to risk dropping him. Once you've got him up in one hand, keep a safety grip on the base of his tail with the other. Gerbils can move fast, especially when they are startled.

To examine your pet, hold him in one hand by encircling his neck with your thumb and forefinger. Extend his body across your palm and tuck his tail between your fourth and fifth fingers to keep him still. Your other hand is left free for doing the examination.

The correct way to hold a gerbil.

Handling and Training

Children should be reminded that gerbils bite when mishandled or provoked.

Biting

For all their docility, gerbils sometimes do bite—but very rarely. In fact, considering that this is their only means of defense, it's remarkable how seldom gerbils do use their teeth. Still, the fact that they are not likely to react violently is no reason to provoke or irritate one. Pushed too far, there's no telling when he will act in self-defense.

Children

Young children need to be introduced to gerbils properly. Otherwise they may get so excited in their delight at handling this soft, wriggly creature that they grasp him too tightly or otherwise hurt the animal, which could result in his nipping. A nip is not a serious thing. Treat it as you would any other cut or scratch—clean it and apply an antiseptic. In the case of a deep bite, you might check with your doctor. (Rabies apparently does not occur in hamsters, gerbils, and other domesticated rodents.) A young child who has been bitten may, however, then become wary of handling small animals. So apply that ounce of prevention by supervising until you are sure that the youngsters and hamsters are accustomed to each other.

Eating from Your Hand

Once your gerbil is used to being held, teach him to accept food from your fingertips. Later on you will use food as a reward for proper behavior. Start by offering long strips of fresh lettuce; you can hold one end while the gerbil nibbles at the other. Gradually use shorter

Handling and Training

Frequent handling enhances the taming process greatly.

pieces. Finally, when he has lost all hesitancy about approaching your fingers, offer him individual sunflower seeds held between your thumb and forefinger.

Playtime

Now you're both ready for some real play. Your gerbil will need a playground, and for this a cardboard box, a plastic wading pool, or a metal tub will be just fine. Then, how about a tunnel, a ladder, a low bridge, steps, slides, swings, or see-saws? Just keep going—as fast as you build them, he'll play with them. Also, a little exploration in strange territory could be fun—in your pockets or other parts of your clothing. But be careful: The gerbil is a rodent, and the word "rodent" comes from the Latin *rodere*, which means to gnaw. Also, don't overdo the play periods: 15- to 20-minute stretches are quite enough.

Some people line their gerbil's toys up on a table top instead of using an enclosure. Gerbils are not afraid of heights, but an excited or startled gerbil can forget his caution for a moment and topple over the edge. A fall of a few feet is not likely to do any harm, but any greater height and your friend is liable to suffer injury.

The Basis of Training

There are a few simple rules to keep in mind when training your gerbil. He has a great deal of curiosity and a relatively short attention span, and these can be real handicaps unless you keep the training periods short. Remove his food an hour before the training session and don't return it until an hour or so afterward. Otherwise you will not be able to use food as an incentive and reward. When you do reward him, make sure you reward

Handling and Training

only correct behavior; if he does not perform properly, don't offer any food or you'll only confuse him.

Train him in stages and keep each stage small. The routine should be simple, and the training sessions should take place at the same time each day. Finally, if you are trying to teach him to respond to a voice command, make it a single-word command, use the same word each time, and try always to pronounce it in the same tone of voice.

Gerbils learn a lot faster than most other rodents but cannot be compared with dogs, cats, or even some birds like parrots. What you can teach them, with a lot of patience and repeated lessons, is to come when they are called, take

food from your hands, press a lever, climb a specific object, enter a specific opening, or approach the cage wall when you tap it with your finger.

Escapees

It is not a good idea to let your gerbils run loose in the house. As I

A simple ledge inside a cage will satisfy the jumping instinct of your pet gerbil.

have said, they can cause damage by gnawing, injure themselves, or get wedged into a crevice. We assume that if your gerbil is loose in your own home there won't be any

A trained gerbil welcomes handling whenever you take him out of the cage.

Handling and Training

hostile cats and dogs around. But how about the possibility of strange ones coming in? And don't forget, there is always the chance that he will fearlessly approach a member of the household and be stepped on before anyone has spotted him.

At some point a gerbil may escape during the play or training sessions. Some experts advise staying put and letting him return to you. If you waggle your fingers near the floor or wave a bit of cloth, he may just come right up to it to see what it's

A gerbil's basic needs are few: food, water, bedding, and if desired an exercise wheel or a few toys.

all about. If this doesn't work, try placing a cardboard mailing tube or similar "tunnel" on the floor near your pet, perhaps baiting it with some of his favorite food. When the wayfarer enters this tunnel, just cup your hands over the ends.

Setting up the cage is a matter of routine from the very start.

44

And Baby Makes Three . . .

For handy reference, here is some basic breeding information about gerbils:

Breeding method: Monogamous (one male and one female per cage).

Sexual maturity: Female, 9 to 12; male, 10 to 12 weeks of age.

Estrus (heat cycle): 4 to 6 days, with a 12- to 15-hour receptive period.

Ovulation: 6 to 10 hours before mating.

Gestation period: 24 to 25 days.

Breeding season: All year around.

Female's weight gain: About 1 ounce.

Litter size: 1 to 12 (average 5).

Male's procreative life: 3 to 24 months.

Female's procreative life: 3 to 20 months, but may continue to mate up to 4 months longer without littering.

Total number of litters: Average about 7.

Breeding frequency: 30 to 40 days.

Longevity: To 3 years.

Before embarking on breeding gerbils, be sure to get information on the breeding requirements of this rodent first.

We don't know whether gerbils are monogamous in the wild, but they are in captivity. Pair them at nine to 12 weeks of age and they'll stay mated for life; in fact, old females are usually reluctant to accept a replacement for a lost mate. While you do hear about one male being bred to two females or even being rotated among several females, females often bully or even kill the male in those situations. For our friend the gerbil a *menage a trois* is decidedly not advisable.

Arranged Marriage

Gerbils seem to prefer to select their own mates, but that is not always possible in captivity, so we

And Baby Makes Three . . .

It is normal for a mother gerbil to move her young about the cage.

do the best we can to pick out the best prospects for our pets.

Gerbil courtship is not too romantic by our standards, but it is fairly noisy and active. The male doesn't seem to be too hard to please; the female is the one who creates the problems. At first she may ward off all advances, and you can expect some sniffing, chasing, and squeaking when the two are first paired, but by the second day the couple is usually cuddled together serenely.

Pair Them Young

Things will run a lot more smoothly if the animals are paired by the age of nine weeks. However, if for one reason or another you cannot get them together while they are young or they seem to be having trouble adjusting to each other, keep them in separate cages side by side until they become somewhat acquainted. If you have only one cage, rig up a temporary divider that will keep them from getting together but through which they can see and converse with each other. If the nuptial cage has been used before, get rid of all the old bedding and wash the cage thoroughly before introducing the new pair; otherwise the odors left by the previous occupants might upset the new inhabitants. Many pairs will not breed unless they have a nesting box. If they seem to be reluctant, provide a nesting box, more retreat areas, or even change the location of the cage to a quieter or more dimly lit area.

The Blessed Event

The majority of matings occur between 5:00 P.M. and early morning; the preferred time is 6:00

And Baby Makes Three . . .

to 8:00 P.M. Repeated matings take place over a period of six to eight hours. The male pursues the female vigorously, pausing every so often to "thump" in a semi-erect position in short staccato bursts. The female sometimes joins him in thumping. There is about a 60% chance of a successful mating within a week after pairing, so don't be surprised if the first litter arrives about a month after the two are first placed together.

Delivery Signs

The fact that the female is busily running around with mouthfuls of bedding to make a nest may be, but is not necessarily, a sign of impending motherhood.

There is no other sign in her behavior that might serve as a signal that something is about to happen. Even the weight change is difficult to detect until just before delivery. If her abdomen looks plump and there are several lumps about the size of small marbles protruding from her sides, you can be reasonably sure that she will deliver in a day or two. Don't be surprised, though, if the first indications you have are the squeaks of the newborn gerbils.

For those of my readers who are parents and remember the late-night rushes to the hospital, it will come as no surprise to learn that most litters are born during the night or very early morning. Only a small percentage occur in the afternoon.

Littering

Delivery is usually uncomplicated and quick—one to two hours, as a rule. Even an inexperienced mother should know what to do. Generally she consumes the placental debris and any stillborn fetuses, but the young that are born alive and die after birth are not usually devoured and should be removed. There is little for you to do during this period if you have already provided ample bedding, food, water, and privacy.

You may furnish some nesting material for shredding. This can be pieces of burlap, soft cloth, cardboard, or ordinary paper—but not tissue paper. Tissue paper may cling to the young and can dehydrate or suffocate them. For the first few days restrain your curiosity and leave the proud parents alone. Disturbing or handling the gerbils might cause them to neglect or harm their young.

And Baby Makes Three . . .

Most books on keeping gerbils usually include a section on the breeding and management of the litter, too.

Post-Partum Heat

Most females go into heat immediately after the birth of a litter, and mating can occur within hours after delivery. As about 85% of such matings are fertile, there is an excellent chance that your gerbils will become parents again in a month or so. However, the implantation of the egg can be somewhat delayed under these circumstances, so that the gestation period may be longer than the normal 24 to 25 days. Of course, there are exceptions, and some females may go several months without producing a litter, especially during cool weather. If the female misses this post-partum period she will not mate again while nursing.

In commercial gerbilries reproductive failures are very rare, occurring in less than 1% of the animals. Unfortunately, this rate is much higher among pet gerbils.

Cannibalism

One difficulty occasionally encountered by breeders of pet rodents is cannibalism by one or both parents. Healthy, properly cared-for gerbils should not be guilty of this practice. The usual causes are insufficient cage space, improper diet (particularly a lack of protein), irregular care, or the owner disturbing the animals when the litter is young. If the male is the culprit, don't be afraid to remove him. The mother will take care of her youngsters very well by herself. The male may be returned to the cage when the young are up and around, but watch him at first to make sure that he doesn't resent them. If he does, separate them again until the babies are out of the cage.

Growth and Development

At birth, our little gerbil friend is only about an inch long, has a stubby tail, and weighs perhaps a tenth of an ounce. Like human babies, he is pink and helpless. His eyes are closed, his ears are folded shut, and he has no teeth. But he can make little mewing sounds, and—although it doesn't get him very far—he can move his limbs.

The fact that gerbils, like most mammals, are born naked is depicted in many books.

Mama's Duties

Mama gerbil arranges the nest, keeps the litter warm, and nurses and washes the babies. If the litter is too large, she may split it into two groups, dividing her time between them, and when the young grow and start to wander, she returns them to the nest.

Papa's Duties

The male is an exemplary parent, especially in comparison to other rodents, though by human standards he leaves a lot to be desired. He does take on some responsibilities like returning strayed young, keeping them warm, washing them, and rearranging the nest—and that's a lot more than a mouse or rat father will do for its young.

The Neglected Litter

We don't really know what prompts an occasional female to neglect her litter. It's possible that if she is too immature or if it is her first litter, she may just not know how to take care of the young. Sometimes her milk supply may be low or of poor quality. But she learns with experience and so will have less trouble nursing a third litter than the first two.

The standard pelleted diet plus water should be adequate to maintain the milk supply throughout the nursing period, but if you think a supplement is necessary, reconstitute some powdered milk or dilute some evaporated milk and give that in the water bottle. Some keepers like to

Growth and Development

Examine closely your young gerbils periodically. Remove any youngster with signs of illness.

add some small amounts of milk-soaked bread to the diet.

Unfortunately, if the mother neglects the litter or if she cannot supply enough milk, the young usually will not survive. Even with larger rodents, scientists have had little success in hand-raising them using substitute mother's milk. However, if there is another gerbil mother handy who has a litter about the same age as yours, she may accept your brood. First place the prospective adoptees atop some of the foster mother's bedding and rub a little of this onto their skin or their backs. Gerbils identify their young by the smell, and a strange odor would upset them.

Lacking another gerbil mother, you could use a white rat if one is available, but be sure you take the same odor precautions. Still, the youngsters are not always accepted by the foster parent, and in that case there is little you can do except to dispose of them as kindly as possible.

As They Grow

Within a few days, color starts to appear, and in a short time the baby has an overall covering of dark gray fur. At about five days the ear flaps unfold. By 12 days the incisors erupt, and soon the gerbils make their first attempt at chewing. By the age of two weeks, the pups have a full coat of smooth dark brown fur and are able to crawl easily, but their eyes still remain shut.

In another week most gerbils' eyes are open. Now they can eat solid food, drink water from a tube, sit, jump, drum their hind feet, and are very active in play or mock fights. The coat has lengthened to the point where it is very much like an adult's but is lighter-colored and not yet as glossy. It would still take two of them to make up an ounce, and their legs are out of proportion to their bodies. The tail is well along

Growth and Development

After breeding, the male parent is usually isolated to prevent unwanted matings from following too soon.

toward the mature length of 90% of the body size.

Weaning

Commercial gerbilries wean the babies when they are 21 to 23 days old in order to make room for the next litter, which could very well arrive when the first is only about 24 days old. Trying to take care of both of them would put quite a strain on the mother's resources.

If you don't think that this is likely to happen in your case, it is possible to leave the family together until the babies are four to five weeks old. A small cage will soon by very crowded. If the litter is large both in numbers and size, when they crowd underneath the mother for their meals they can literally lift her up into the air!

Before you remove them completely from the mother, be sure that the young can eat solid food and drink water. Gradually add ground pellets, some breakfast cereal, and maybe some milk-soaked bits of bread to their diet—the latter with a sprinkling of sugar, perhaps, to ensure ready acceptance.

Separate the Sexes

If you have room, cage the sexes separately. Allow 15 to 20 square inches of floor space for each gerbil at first. While gerbils do not grow as fast as mice or rats, their weight will still double between the ages of three weeks and eight weeks, by which time they will weigh about 1¼ ounces. By the time they are eight weeks old each should have about 50 square inches of floor space. If you have not already done so, you must separate the sexes by age ten weeks in order to prevent brother-sister matings, as inbreeding is generally considered undesirable.

By the time he is 12 weeks old, the average gerbil weighs about 2 ounces and is sexually mature. By five months of age the gerbil has reached full size, about 3 ounces, although some males weigh as much as 4 ounces.

Keep Him Healthy

A healthy gerbil does not mind being handled unless it experiences pain from an incorrect way of holding.

Although infectious diseases are relatively common among most rodents, gerbils are, happily, an exception. Given reasonably safe and sanitary conditions, they should never suffer from any pneumonia-like respiratory diseases or enteritis (diarrhea). In fact, it is unusual for gerbils to succumb to *any* disease after weaning age, and chances are you will never have occasion to use the information given here.

Minor Injuries

Scratches or cuts rarely occur when a pair of gerbils are caged together, but when a group of mature animals is confined to the same area, fighting and injury may result. If the injuries are minor, they'll heal without treatment. Of course, you should separate the combatants to prevent further injuries. If you feel an antiseptic is necessary, apply something mild like rubbing alcohol or peroxide. You can clean the area with a mild soap and water, flush it well, dry it thoroughly, and keep the gerbil on flat paper rather than his regular bedding until it is healed—dusty bedding might infect the open area. Before using antiseptics like Mercurochrome or tincture of iodine, bear in mind that a gerbil licks himself during grooming, so apply only a minimal amount. If the injury is extensive, it is best to consult a veterinarian.

Delivery Problems

Females will occasionally die during delivery due to pelvic obstruction. There is no way of foretelling this. Sometimes gerbils do not live to weaning age because

Keep Him Healthy

they are runts or because of a condition characterized by a balding on the upper part of the body. The causes are unknown, and there is very little that can be done about these abnormalities. Sometimes early weaning (at three weeks) will save them by reducing the competition and preventing bullying by littermates.

You can expect your gerbil to stay well when provided with its basic needs.

Tyzzer's Disease

This is probably caused by a microscopic parasite of the genus *Bacillus* occasionally found in rabbits, mice, and rats. It is a puzzling disease, because the infected animal can apparently carry the parasite a long time without any noticeable symptoms until something triggers the disease. So far as I know, only one group of gerbils has ever become infected. The animals huddled in cage corners, had rough coats, ate little, and lost weight. The infection may very well be spread via the animals' droppings; it can be transmitted to other rodents via bedding, so infected animals must be isolated. Otherwise it might be best to destroy them to prevent the spread of the infection. Tyzzer's disease can only be transmitted to closely related rodents.

Vitamin Deficiency

If your gerbil seems to be losing his appetite, has weight loss, loses hair, arches his back, walks with a wobbly gait, and has a rough coat, chances are he is suffering from a deficiency of thiamine (vitamin B_1). If you have been feeding the

53

Keep Him Healthy

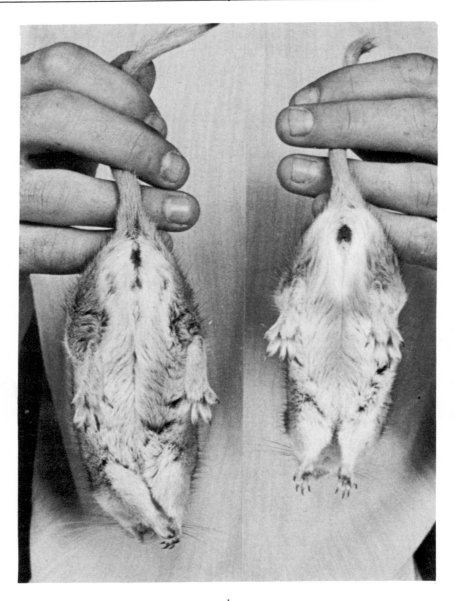

A male gerbil. | A female gerbil.

Keep Him Healthy

A water bottle anchored outside of the cage can be removed without your having to lift the upper half of the cage.

recommended pelleted diet and keeping the food fresh, this should not occur. Supplementing his diet by putting water-soluble multivitamins into the drinking water is one way of preventing vitamin B deficiency.

You may have noticed your gerbils eating their droppings. Many animals do this. The practice, called coprophagy, may be necessary for their health. The droppings are rich in B vitamins which are manufactured by bacteria in the animals' digestive tract.

Seizures

Moving an animal and sometimes even routine handling causes a strain on him. Occasionally this can result in a seizure that can range anywhere from a hypnotic-like state to a series of convulsions (twitching and jerking). The cause may be a hereditary defect that interferes with normal blood circulation in the brain when the animal is under stress. Generally the condition lasts only a few minutes; the animal then returns to normal with no apparent harm. No treatment is indicated.

Ulcerations

Ulceration (red rawness) on the nose or mouth, often accompanied by some hair loss, is a very common and minor ailment that responds

Keep Him Healthy

Many gerbils in captivity succumb from neglect rather than disease.

readily to treatment with local antiseptics. It is probably due to abrasions—caused by intense burrowing—that later become infected. Be sure that all the interior cage surfaces are smooth, and keep the bedding soft, dry, and clean.

Hair Loss

Sometimes a pet gerbil will lose hair from the upper part of the nose with no concomitant redness or rawness. This may be simply the result of rubbing up against the bars while poking his nose through to chew the cage grid. Occasionally the hair of a gerbil's tail will become sparse or even drop out entirely in

areas near its base. This may be due to another gerbil nibbling at it and seems to occur more frequently when the animals are crowded together. The answer is to allow more space for each individual; if that doesn't work, they may have to be separated.

There is some evidence to indicate that hair loss may be due to a deficiency of a B-complex vitamin known as para amino benzoic acid, or PABA for short. This is available in tablet form. Just crush a tablet and mix some in with the food and see if this doesn't help. Again, adding vitamins to the drinking water may be the answer.

Captions for color pages 57-64:

Page 57: Two dove gerbils and a cinnamon gerbil near a favorite toy; all are young animals. Page 58: A normally colored gerbil in closeup; note the comparative largeness of the eye. Page 59: White gerbil inquisitively sniffing flowers. Page 60: Light dove and cinnamon gerbils preening. Page 61: Pet gerbils treated well can soon learn to climb right onto an owner's hand to eat sunflower seeds. Page 62: Above: Baby gerbils at an age of five days. Below: The same babies at an age of ten days. Page 63: Note the tuft of hair at the tip of the tail of this white gerbil; the tuft is not characteristic of any other pet rodent. Page 64: Mother gerbil and her young; even the most docile female gerbil can be combative when she's guarding and nursing her young.

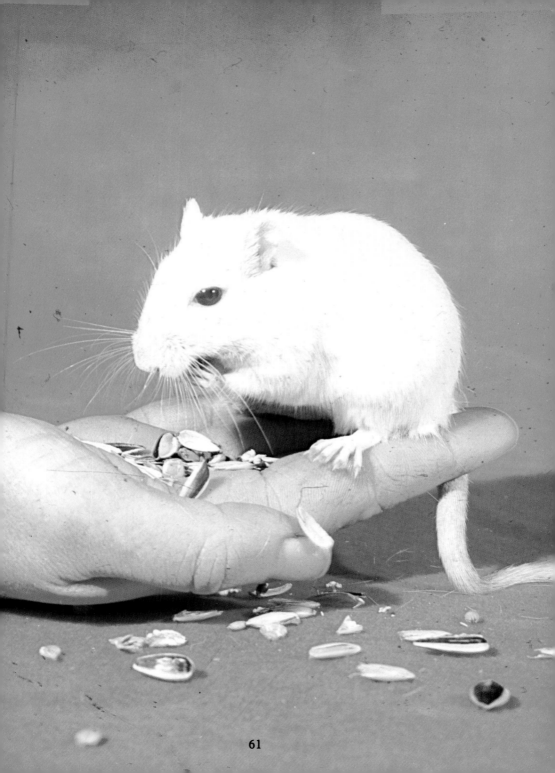

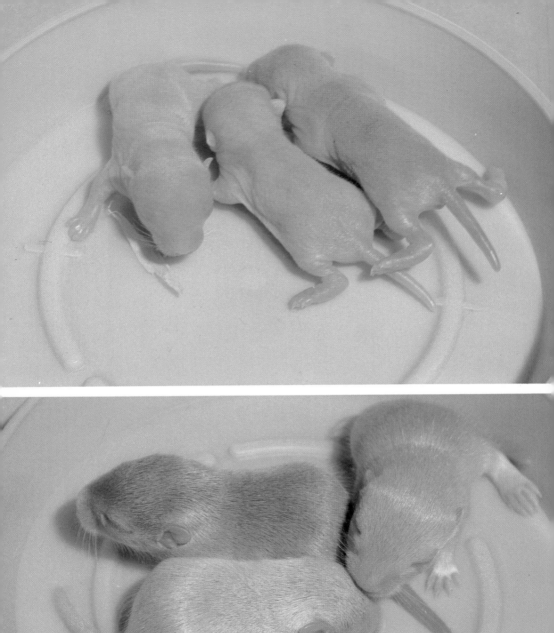

Keep Him Healthy

Keep the family cat away from the gerbil's cage. Seeing a natural enemy at close range can be traumatic.

External Parasites

Gerbils are relatively free of these pests—if your pet has any, chances are he caught them from another animal. Check with your veterinarian, although as a general rule you can use the same insecticidal powder marketed for cats or hamsters. Dog flea powders are not usually suitable; because dogs do not lick themselves, products are often used for them that would be harmful to cats, gerbils, and hamsters, who will ingest some of the material during self-grooming. Young gerbils are extremely sensitive to insecticides.

A piece of flea collar that is marketed for pets may be hung near the gerbil's cage (safely out of the animal's reach, of course); the vapors it exudes will act as a very effective pesticide.

Keep Him Healthy

Miscellaneous

Old gerbils, like most other aging animals in captivity, tend to put on weight. At first it was thought that this might be due to a form of diabetes, but subsequent research disproved this theory. If your gerbil becomes overweight, try cutting down his food supply.

Cedar wood shavings will keep the cage sweet-smelling for a period of time.

Sometimes the eyes of an older gerbil may protrude excessively and the eyelids become inflamed. The cause and cure are unknown.

Keep Him Clean

See that your gerbil's food and water are fresh and uncontaminated

Examine the air vents of the cage occasionally. Keep these openings free of dust and other material for good air circulation.

by insects, wild rodents, or harmful chemicals. Wash and disinfect the cage, water bottle, and other equipment every month or so—any standard household disinfectant will do. Make sure the cage and accessories are thoroughly rinsed and dried before the animals are returned to their home. If you use a spray disinfectant, be certain that the animals are outside its range.

A Friend to Science

Since his arrival in the United States, the gerbil has earned a permanent place on the list of laboratory rodents, having been used in a wide range of biomedical research from A (aerospace medicine) to Z (Zoonoses—communicable diseases between animals and man). In fact, one veterinarian calls the gerbil the research rodent of the future.

Some of the findings made by scientists have been passed along in the form of good advice found in books.

The Unique Gerbil

A number of characteristics are unique to the gerbil. He is the only laboratory animal capable of body temperature regulation over a wide range of higher temperatures. His ability to manufacture water from dry foods and to produce highly concentrated urine are also being studied. In addition, researchers have learned that gerbils can withstand about twice the amount of radiation that common rodents can tolerate, and they would like to determine whether such protective mechanisms can be applicable for humans. All of these characteristics may be significant in solving some of the problems facing man in future prolonged space flights.

Cholesterol and Heart Disease

Even when fed a diet containing a normal percentage of fats, gerbils develop high cholesterol levels in their blood. This might lead one to believe that increasing the fats in the diet would create problems, but they evidently have a protective mechanism or special pathway in their bodies for handling fat so that even increased levels of fat don't bother them. Unfortunately, man is not as lucky as the gerbil in that respect—that is, there seems to be some relationship between increased dietary fats and a higher level of fats in man's circulatory system, and these are implicated in heart disease. By studying the gerbil man might learn how to handle disorders related to excess fat in the arteries.

A Friend to Science

Tameness is a quality that can be lost unless reinforced by frequent handling.

Hormone Studies

The prominent sebaceous gland on the gerbil's belly is a unique aid for studying the influence of hormones on glandular development, and gerbils played a part in the development of contraceptives.

Neurology

Neurologists report that gerbils are useful in studies of blood vessels supplying the brain, seizure activity, the visual system, and brain damage.

Dentistry

Dental researchers tell us that gerbils are susceptible to diseases affecting the structure that supports the teeth and also to cavities. They hope by introducing the "bugs" that cause tooth decay to learn how cavities develop.

Tissue Transplants

Transplanting tissues and organs from one animal to another has been in the news in recent years, and there has been much discussion of cases of tissue rejection (when the body of the receiver rejects tissue or an organ from a strange donor). Hamsters and gerbils are the only small mammals so far to show considerable tolerance in accepting foreign tissue grafts even from randomly bred animals.

Transplanting tissues from one animal to another is important not only to replace diseased organs or parts but also in studying cancer, endocrine functions, and, of course, the very factors that cause rejection.

A Friend to Science

Psychological Studies

Gerbils are docile, curious, socially oriented, and highly territorial—in short, extremely suitable subjects for psychological research. At one university alone, six investigators are studying the gerbil's behavior to see how these traits evolved.

Studies have been going on for years to determine how much effect the environment in which a child is raised has on his intelligence. Of course, people cannot be put into laboratories and subjected to experiments, but we can select different environments. Gerbils isolated in a dull environment as opposed to those exposed to stimulating objects show that the brain is affected by the animals' experiences in their environment. The results suggest that gerbils might be useful in determining what amount of social contact is desirable for good mental health.

Standing on its haunches is characteristic of many rodents, including the gerbil.

And That's Not All . . .

The gerbil is valuable in the investigation of many diseases affecting man, including tuberculosis, rabies, bubonic plague, polio, and anthrax. They are also susceptible to many parasitic diseases affecting man and domestic animals. One of these diseases, schistosomiasis (bilharzia), affects about 150 million people in tropical areas. We should be proud of our little gerbil's role in the campaign against this major affliction.

Gerbils in the Classroom

Gerbils are great pets, and children need not be limited to enjoying them at home. It's also lots of fun and educational to watch and study animals in the classroom, and teachers know that of all animals, small, furry creatures are the most attention-getting. Gerbils, in fact, are probably the ideal classroom mammals for the same reasons they are ideal pets. They are small, clean, easy to handle, and need only a minimum of care. Because they are so lively, they make perfect subjects for animal behavior studies, and many experiments can be duplicated by the students at home. It's not surprising, then, that suppliers have been receiving large orders for gerbils from public and private schools!

Children can often bring their gerbils and housing to the classroom as a class project.

Public Housing

In general, my suggestions for housing pet gerbils at home may be applied to the classroom. More housing space should be provided, however, in order to give the class a better look at the animals' activity. If you have a small bookcase, just arrange a wire mesh front, cut holes in the shelves, build ladder "stairways" leading from one story to the next, and you have a gerbil apartment house.

Fitted with grid tops, large aquariums or metal tubs are quite satisfactory. And for a classroom project, the students can simulate a gerbil's natural habitat using a dampened mixture of one part sand to two parts soil for burrowing. Live grass and plants can be added as well, but you must still furnish the basic diet and a water bottle. Heat, light, and humidity can be controlled to suit the gerbil's preferences.

Gerbils in the Classroom

Handling the docile little fellow in the classroom is not a special problem, although younger children must always be supervised to prevent rough handling. Don't hold the animal too high in the air, as a fall might injure or kill him. You can put identifying marks on the tops of their heads with a marking pen or food or hair dye. But separate the animals until the markings are dry to keep them from licking one another.

The Scientific Approach

Here are a few tips to help you keep your classroom experiments scientifically controlled. First of all, remember that the animals will react to your presence. To reduce or eliminate this possibility, you will want to suppress any "cues" that the gerbils might sense that might influence their behavior. For example, to eliminate distracting movements, cover the front of the enclosure with one-way aluminized foil (like a one-way mirror) that you can obtain at very low cost in scientific supply houses.

Sounds may be minimized by surrounding the cage with insulating baffles or a soundproofing material, but make certain to allow for adequate ventilation. Odors can be masked by washing the apparatus between tests or by providing a constant flow of air. The latter is easy: all you need is a small fan blowing from the cage toward you. Be careful—if it is blowing from you toward the cage it will carry your odor to the gerbil and defeat its purpose.

Many modern zoos take advantage of the fact that animals have poor "red" vision. They do this by keeping the building dark and

A display of toys and treats for gerbils and other mammals is a feature common to most petshops.

71

Gerbils in the Classroom

illuminating the cages with red light. This creates a nighttime atmosphere for the animals, who are normally active then. When the building is closed to visitors, a daytime atmosphere is created by turning on the lights, and of course many of the animals go to sleep during this period. You can do the same thing with your gerbils by using a red light or by covering the cage with red cellophane. (Don't forget the ventilation.)

Plan Ahead

Successful experiments depend heavily, of course, on successful planning for gathering and recording information, for the design and construction of equipment, standardization of tests, and data interpretation. Whether you are a teacher or student you will find that planning the experiment can be just as challenging as the study itself.

Experiments with Food

To measure food consumption, feed only dry pellets from a hopper, weighing the initial amount and then reweighing after seven days.

Always have a spare package of gerbil food for emergencies. Bad weather conditions or other unforeseen causes may prevent you from leaving your house to get gerbil food.

The difference will be the approximate consumption level (although there will be some waste). You can also study food preferences by placing equal amounts of two different foods side by side and observing which is eaten first. Then compare that "favorite" with a third kind of food. You may want to test again later on to see whether the gerbil's tastes have changed.

Gerbils in the Classroom

New housing products for pet gerbils are featured on a dealer's display table.

Bodily Functions

An inexpensive stethoscope will enable you to hear a gerbil's rapid heartbeat. Use a watch to estimate its pulse rate; compare it with yours. Count the breaths taken by a resting gerbil in a given time; determine its respiration rate and compare it with yours. Also, compare the respiration of a gerbil at rest with the rate after he has been on an exercise wheel for a little while.

Gerbils in the Classroom

Activity

How hard do gerbils work and play? One way to gauge activity is to mount a mechanical counter or tally register on an exercise wheel; see how the number of revolutions changes according to time of day, sex and age of the animals, and the duration of the active periods.

Being taught how to put together a maze of tunnels from a kit.

There are many other questions that can be answered in classroom experiments: How small a hole can a gerbil squeeze through? What thickness of paper does he prefer for shredding into nesting material? How do gerbils behave in a maze?

Be Observant

To catalog various gerbil activities and the percentage of time devoted to each, you will need a tape recorder or a team of observers plus a metronome or hand signal to indicate the passage of each second of time for five minutes. Then the chief observer watches the gerbil's activities and calls out the major kind of activity at each second—social contact, exploration, alert posture, resting, eating, grooming. The recorded notes or tape will enable you to figure the results.

Mice and rats tend to hug the walls when allowed their freedom in an open area. Do gerbils? Mark the bottom of a box 3 to 4 feet on a side into 4- or 6-inch squares, letter them

These tubes split apart for easy cleaning and storage. They snap back to create a tunnel-like tube.

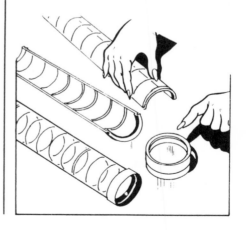

74

Gerbils in the Classroom

in one direction, and number them in the other. Now place a gerbil in the center and count the total number of squares he enters into in a period of three to five minutes. Have another person trace the gerbil's path during this period on graph paper, with squares corresponding to those on the box floor. The sketch will give an idea of the exploratory movements, and a string can be used to measure the scale distance covered. The number of squares entered is also an indication of exploratory activity. You can compare results with

One can buy add-ons individually or as many as desired. This is limited only by the amount of money and space you have.

different ages, sexes, or other species if available.

The Maze

How do gerbils behave in a maze? You can make a simple maze, T- or Y-shaped, with side walls, or an elevated maze without walls. Or you can design a more complex maze.

Here's to the Gerbil!

One child psychologist believes that children not only enjoy pets, but they also actually need pets if they are to grow up into normal, functioning adult human beings. While this may be stretching a point, there is no doubt that the value of pet ownership extends beyond the obvious pleasure it gives a child. The experience of pet ownership with all its responsibilities, the relationship of mutual affection and trust between pet and master, and the many lessons to be learned about himself and others from the animal's behavior—these all are invaluable to a child.

In these days of increasing urbanization, there is less and less open space, and apartments are getting smaller and smaller. This limits our choice of a pet. Dogs and cats are great, but often there just isn't room for them, and many housing developments prohibit their being kept on the premises. Tropical fishes, goldfish, birds—these too are fine pets. But children, with their highly developed tactile curiosity, need a creature they can hold, touch, pet, and cuddle; and in many cases it's also got to be something that Mother won't object to, that won't offend the neighbors, and that Dad won't have to walk at night when he comes home tired. Our little friend the gerbil fits this bill perfectly.

Besides, gerbils are not just children's pets—they're people pets. Their harmonious marital partnership and exemplary child-rearing ways can serve as a lesson to all of us. Their sweet, trusting nature endears them to adults from all walks of life.

It is worthwhile having spare cages on hand for isolating breeders or sick gerbils.

So here's to the gerbil: Long may he flourish and the cult of the gerbil spread throughout the land. Sweet, modest, lively, and friendly, he works his way into the hearts of all with whom he comes in contact. Truly it can be said of the gerbil, "To know him is to love him."

Suggested Reading

As gerbils become more popular as pets, more products will be especially designed for the comfort of this well-behaved rodent.

Your pet shop will have many other books about gerbils. T.F.H. publishes the following recommended books.

THE T.F.H. BOOK OF GERBILS
By Mrs. M. Ostrow
ISBN 0-87666-824-4
T.F.H. HP-009
Contents: Introduction. The Gerbil. Feeding. Housing. Selecting Breeding Stock. Breeding Behavior. Selective Breeding. Health Care.

Details of gerbil behavior possibly puzzling to the amateur pet-keeper are clearly explained in this book. The many attractive, varied colors available to knowledgeable breeders are splendidly portrayed in lively photographs.
Hard cover, 8½ × 11"; 64 pages
49 full-color photos.

THE ENCYCLOPEDIA OF GERBILS
By D. Robinson
ISBN 0-87666-915-1
TFH H-974
Contents: Covers the Set-Up and Maintenance of Housing Facilities, Handling, Feeding, Breeding, and Care of Gerbils. It is also a comprehensive guide to the gerbil's characteristics and behavior.
Hard cover, 8 × 5½; 224 pages
57 full-color photos, 102 black and white photos

Index

Age, 11
Anthrax, 69

Barley, 37
Bedding, 25, 26
Biting, 41
Bread, 37
Bubonic plague, 69

Cage, hamster, 15
Cages, plastic, 13
Cages, steel, 13
Cannibalism, 48
Cats, 43
Children and gerbils, 76
Cholesterol, 67
Circadian rhythm, 35
Clover, 39
Corn, 37
Cornflakes, 37
Courtship, 46
Crackers, 37

Dandelion, 39
Dangers, 34
Deer mouse, 8
Dentistry, 68
Diet, 37
Dog Biscuits, 37
Dogs, 43
Dry foods, 37
   Seeds, 37

Enteritis (diarrhea), 52
Estrus (heat cycle), 45
Exercise, 28

Flea collar, 65
Fruits & vegetables, 38

Gerbils, class project, 70-71
Gerbils in Science, 67-69
Gerbils as laboratory animals, 67
Gerbils in zoos, 71
Gestation period, 45, 48
Guinea Pig, 5

Hair loss, 56
Hamster, 5, 8, 35, 38
Handling, 40
Hormone stuelies, 68
Heart disease, 67
Humidity, 33

Injuries, 52
Insecticides, 65
Insects, 39

Jerboa, 7

Kangaroo, 8

Longevity, 45

Index

Meadow mouse, 8
Meriones unguiculatus, 7
Mouse, 5, 49

Nest Box, 28
Neurology, 68
Newspaper, as bedding material, 26
Noise, 33

Oatmeal, 37
Ovulation, 45

Parasites, external, 65
Parrots, 43
Peanuts, 37
Pellets, 37
  Guinea pig, 37
Pelvic obstruction, 53
Polio, 69
Popcorn, 37
Post-partum heat, 48
Potato chips, 37
Pseudo/false pregnancy, 11
Psychological studies, 69

Rabies, 69
Rat, 6, 35, 49, 50
Respiratory diseases, 52

Schistosomiasis, 69
Schwentker, Dr. Victor, 7
Sebaceous gland, 8

Seizures, 55
Sexing, 11
Sexual maturity, 45
Shepherds purse, 39
Squash seeds, 37
Sunflower seeds, 37

Temperature, 32
Tissue transplants, 69
Toys, 28, 42
Training, 42
Tuberculosis, 69
Tyzzers disease, 53

Ulcerations, 55

Vitamin deficiency, 53
Voles, 8

Water, 27
Weaning, 51
West Foundation, 7
Wooden Cage, 16

Yarrow, 39